READING POWER

High-Tech Vehicles

BROADNECK ELEMENTARY
MEDIA CENTER

Cruise Ships

William Amato

The Rosen Publishing Group's
PowerKids Press™
New York

Published in 2002 by The Rosen Publishing Group, Inc.
29 East 21st Street, New York, NY 10010

First Edition

Book Design: Brian Stone

Photo Credits: Cover, pp. 4–5, 8, 16–17, 18, 19 (top), 19 (bottom), 21 © Royal Caribbean; p. 7 © Key Color/IndexStock; p. 9 © Hulton-Deutsch Collection/Corbis; pp. 10–11 © Mark Gibson/IndexStock; pp. 12–13 © Photri-Microstock; p. 14 © Barry Winiker/IndexStock; p. 15 (top) © Paul A. Souders/Corbis; p. 15 (bottom) © Jeff Greenberg/Photri-Microstock

Amato, William.
Cruise ships / William Amato.
     p. cm. — (High-tech vehicles)
Includes bibliographical references and index.
ISBN 0-8239-6010-2 (library binding)
1. Cruise ships—Juvenile literature. I. Title.
VM381 .A46 2001
623.8'2432—dc21

                                        2001000277

Manufactured in the United States of America

Contents

Cruise Ships

Cruise ships are large boats. They are like hotels on the water. Cruise ships travel all over the world. They stop at many interesting places.

Size of Cruise Ships

Ship Size	Number of People
Small	50–799
Medium	800–1,499
Large	1,500–2,299
Mega	2,300 or more

Building Cruise Ships

Cruise ships are built in dry docks. A dry dock is a place with no water where ships are made. Large cranes are used to build cruise ships. When a ship is finished, it is put into the water.

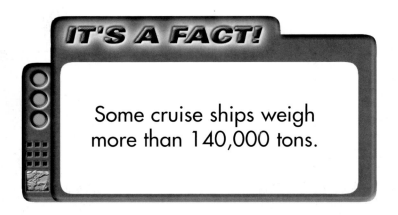

IT'S A FACT!

Some cruise ships weigh more than 140,000 tons.

This cruise ship is in a dry dock.

Running Cruise Ships

Cruise ships have very big engines. The engines spin the propellers. The propellers move the ship.

Cruise ship engines

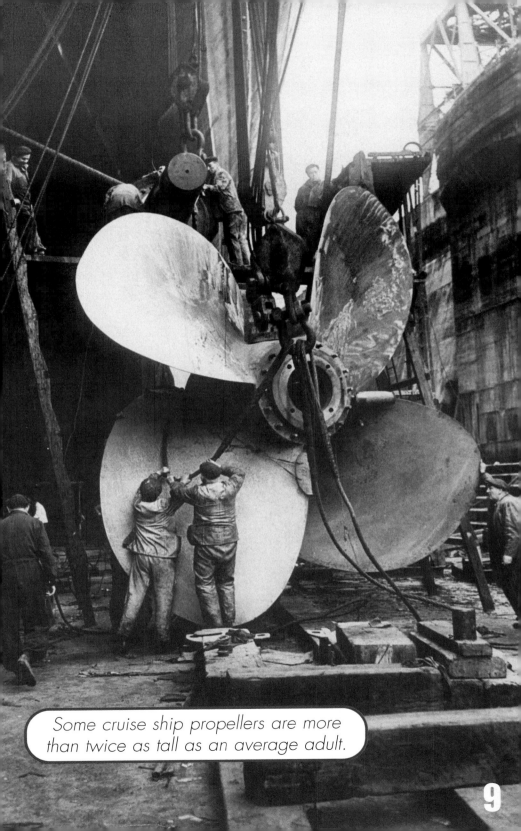

Some cruise ship propellers are more than twice as tall as an average adult.

9

The bridge is where the captain works. The bridge has many computers. Computers help the captain and the crew run the ship.

IT'S A FACT!

A ship's computers are so smart that they can steer the ship without the captain's help.

The radio room is where the ship's crew can talk to crews on other ships. Crew members can also call ahead to the places where they are going.

The Crew

There are many different jobs on a cruise ship. The chief engineer keeps the ship running. Painters keep the ship looking new. Pursers help people stay safe and have fun.

Chief engineer

Painters

Purser

Eating on a cruise ship is like eating at a fancy restaurant. Chefs in large kitchens make meals for the people.

IT'S A FACT!

Some cruise ships serve pizza 24 hours a day. The chefs can make about 800 pizzas a day.

17

Having Fun

There are many places to have fun on a cruise ship. Some ships have ice skating rinks and basketball courts. You can even go rock climbing on some cruise ships.

When the cruise ends, the ship comes back to the harbor. Traveling on a cruise ship can be a great way to see many places in the world.

Glossary

bridge (brihj) the place where the captain runs the ship

cranes (kraynz) machines with long, swinging arms that lift and move heavy objects

cruise (krooz) a trip on a ship that usually includes stops at several places

harbor (har-buhr) a body of water near land where a ship docks

mega (meg-uh) very large in size

propellers (pruh-pehl-uhrz) metal parts with spinning blades that help a ship move

purser (puhr-suhr) the person who helps people on a cruise ship

steer (steer) to guide a ship

Resources

Books

Look Inside Cross-Sections: Ships
by Moira Butterfield and Jonothan Potter
Dorling Kindersley Publishing (1994)

Boats and Ships
by Jason Cooper
Rourke Enterprises (1991)

Web Site

The Oceanliner Museum
http://www.oceanliner.org/index.htm

Index

Word Count: 281

Note to Librarians, Teachers, and Parents

If reading is a challenge, Reading Power is a solution! Reading Power is perfect for readers who want high-interest subject matter at an accessible reading level. These fact-filled, photo-illustrated books are designed for readers who want straightforward vocabulary, engaging topics, and a manageable reading experience. With clear picture/text correspondence, leveled Reading Power books put the reader in charge. Now readers have the power to get the information they want and the skills they need in a user-friendly format.